Sight Words Word Search for Kids Ages 4-8

Disclaimer

Copyright © 2022

All Rights Reserved.

No part of this book can be transmitted or reproduced in any form including print, electronic, photocopying, scanning, mechanical or recording without prior written permission from the author.

While the author has taken utmost efforts to ensure the accuracy of the written content, all readers are advised to follow information mentioned herein at their own risk. The author cannot be held responsible for any personal or commercial damage caused by information. All readers are encouraged to seek professional advice when needed.

Pre-K

Puzzle 1

An   Away   Find
Help   Me   One
Said   Two   Where

Puzzle 2

And   Come   Down
For   Go   Little
Play   The   To
Up

Puzzle 3

Blue   Here   Jump

Look   My   Not

Run   We   you

Puzzle 4

Big Can Funny
In Is It
Make Red See
Three

Puzzle 5

An   Come   Down

Help   In   Look

Make   Play   To

Puzzle 6

Big   Here   Is

It   Little   Red

Run   Where

Puzzle 7

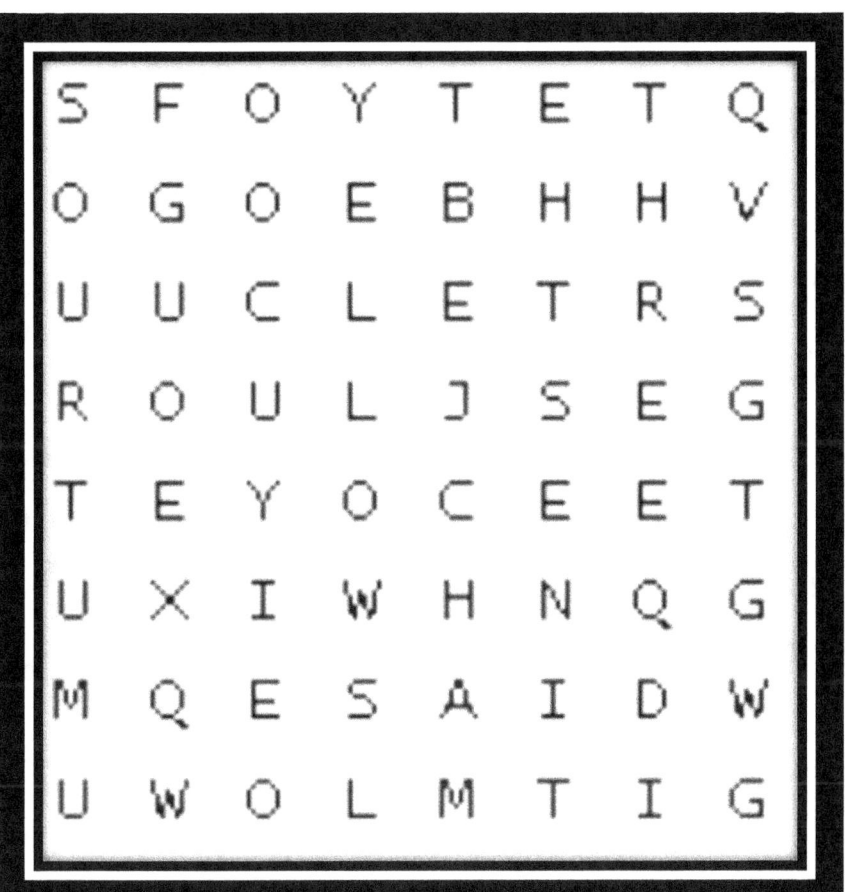

bulb   go   said
see   the   three
we   Yellow   you

Puzzle 8

And	Can	Find
For	Jump	Not
One	Two	Up

Puzzle 9

Away   Funny   Me

My

Kindergarten

Puzzle #10

Are   Ate   But
Say   Soon   They
This   Too   Was

Puzzle #11

Black   Do   Eat
Have   Our   Please
Pretty   Went   What

Puzzle #12

Am   Four   Get

On   Saw   That

There   Well   Will

Puzzle #13

All	At	Came
He	Like	Must
Ride	Under	White

Puzzle #14

Be   Did   New

No   Now   Ran

She   So   Yes

Puzzle #15

Brown   Good   Into

Out   Want   Who

With

Puzzle #16

P	R	M	E	Z	M	S	U
V	Q	M	N	U	N	B	K
X	A	P	S	M	A	S	L
C	Y	T	T	E	R	P	T
F	T	H	E	R	E	S	H
D	A	A	T	C	I	R	I
E	V	A	H	I	H	D	S
H	I	O	E	W	W	K	E

Came	Have	Must
Pretty	Ran	Ride
There	This	With

Puzzle #17

Are   Ate   Eat

Four   Into   Our

That   Well   What

Puzzle #18

Did   Good   Saw

Say   Too   Went

Who   Will   Yes

Puzzle #19

At
Get
Soon

Be
Please
Under

Do
She
Was

Puzzle #20

Am   But   He

No   Now   On

Out   They   Want

Puzzle #21

All   Black   Brown
Like   New   So
White

First Grade

Puzzle #22

Any   From   Give
Live   Of   Open
Round   Take   When

Puzzle #23

Could Had His
How Let Once
Over Stop Thank

Puzzle #24

An	By	Him
Just	May	Them
Think	Walk	Were

Puzzle #25

Ask		Every		Going	
Has		Her		Know	
Put		Some		Then	

Puzzle #26

After   Again   As

Fly   Old

Puzzle #27

After   Ask   Going

Know   Live   Open

Put   Take   Were

Puzzle #28

Again   An   Him
Over   Round   Some
Thank   Think   Walk

Puzzle #29

As   By   Fly
From   How   Just
Of   Old   Then

Puzzle #30

Any	Give	Had
Has	Her	His
Let	May	Stop

Puzzle #31

Could   Every   Once

Them   when

Second Grade
Puzzle #32

Always   Around   Because
Been   Before   Best
Both   Buy   Call

Puzzle #33

Cold   Does   Don't
fast   first   five
found   gave   Goes

Puzzle #34

green   its   made
many   off   or
pull   read   right

Puzzle #35

sing   sit   sleep
tell   their these
those   upon   us

Puzzle #36

use   very   wash
which why   wish
work would write
your

Third Grade
Puzzle #37

Better   Cut   Grow
Hot   If   Keep
never   show   ten

Puzzle #38

A	L	Z	F	P	E	S	N
G	B	E	P	I	D	W	L
T	N	O	C	C	O	S	L
T	R	I	U	K	E	H	A
M	G	Y	R	T	V	O	M
F	U	L	L	B	Z	E	S
T	O	D	A	Y	T	G	L
R	E	H	T	E	G	O	T

About   Bring   Full
own   pick   small
today   together   try

Puzzle #39

Drink   Eight   Far
Hold   Hurt   myself
only   start   warm

Puzzle #40

Carry Draw Got
laugh light Long
much shall six

Puzzle #41

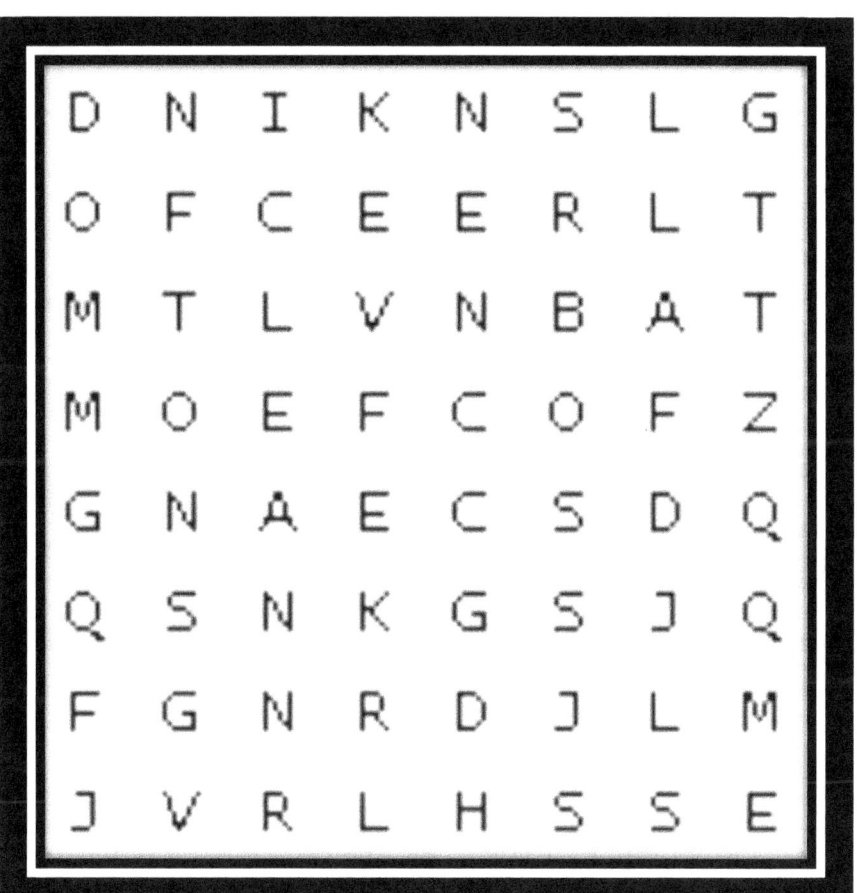

Clean   Done   Fall

Kind   seven

Puzzle #42

Better   Draw   Hurt

Kind   light   only

seven   six   Ten

Puzzle #43

About	Done	Full
Grow	laugh	myself
own	show	together

Puzzle #44

Bring   Drink   Got

Hot   much   never

pick   small   today

Puzzle #45

Eight   Fall   Far
Hold   If   long
start   try   warm

Puzzle #47

Carry Clean Cut

Keep shall

Noun
Puzzle #48

Apple   Boat   Corn
Floor   Home   Kitty
Pig   Snow   Wind

Puzzle #49

Bed   Bird   Coat
Doll   Ground   Letter
Mother   Toy   Window

Puzzle #50

Cake	Chicken	Dog
Morning	Name	Party
School	Street	Wood

Puzzle #51

Baby	Bell	Day
Eye	Father	Fish
Leg	Rain	Sister

Puzzle #52

Ball   Car   Cat

Children   Fire   Picture

Rabbit   Ring

Puzzle #53

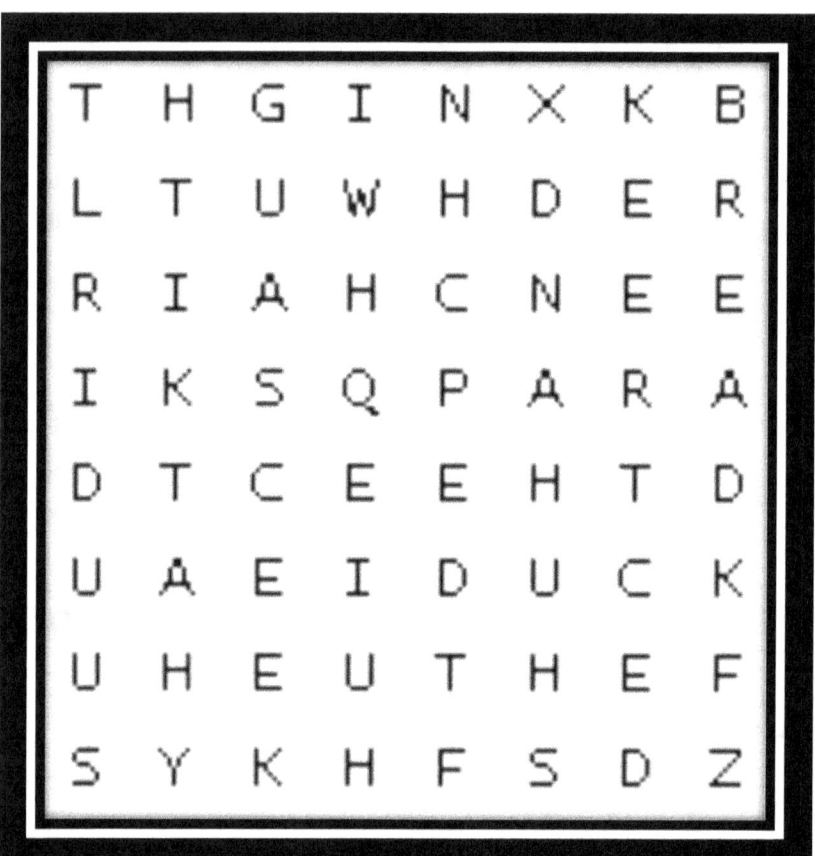

Bread	Chair	Duck
Hand	Head	Night
Sheep	Stick	Tree

Puzzle #54

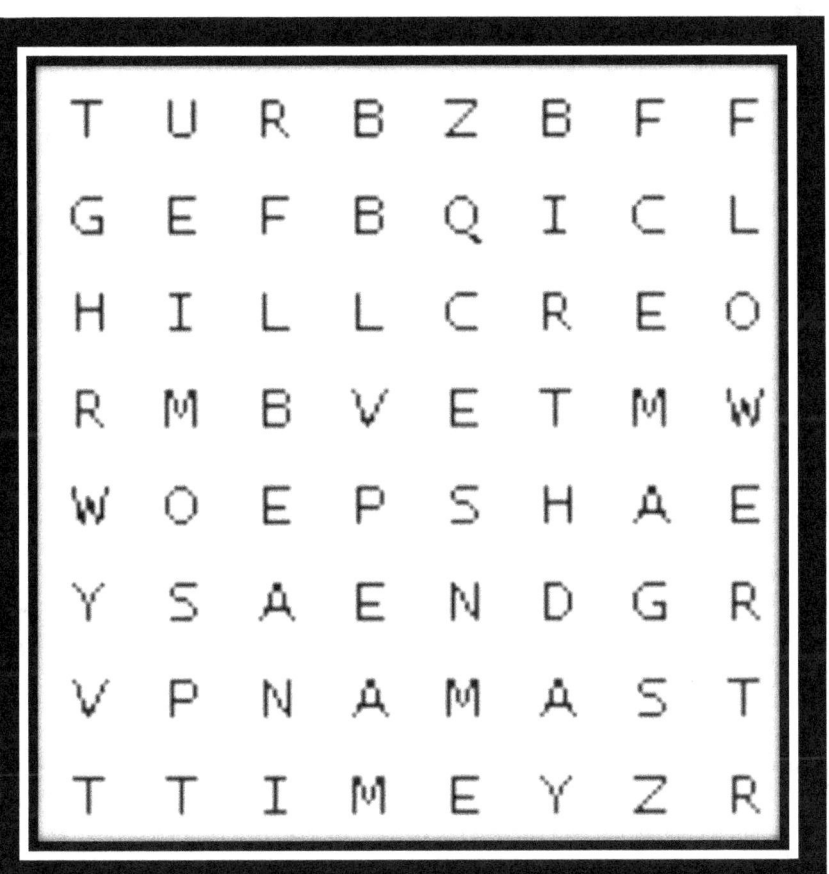

Birthday   Boy   Flower
Game   Hill   Man
Nest   Paper   Time

Puzzle #55

Brother Door Farmer
Feet   Men   Shoe
Table   Thing Water

Puzzle #56

Bear   Box   Farm
Garden   Goodbye   House
Robin   Sun   Watch

Puzzle #57

Back   Egg   Grass
Milk   Seed   Song
Top

Puzzle #58

Cow   Girl   Horse
Money   Way

Noun 2
Puzzle #59

Birthday   Day   Game
Ground   Night   Sheep
Top   Wood

Puzzle #60

Coat		Eye		Letter
Paper		Rain		Ring
Shoe		Sister		Tree

Puzzle #61

Bear   Bread   Father
Goodbye   Name   Table
Time   Watch

Puzzle #62

Boy   Brother   Chair
Head   Home   Men
Party   Street   Water

Puzzle #63

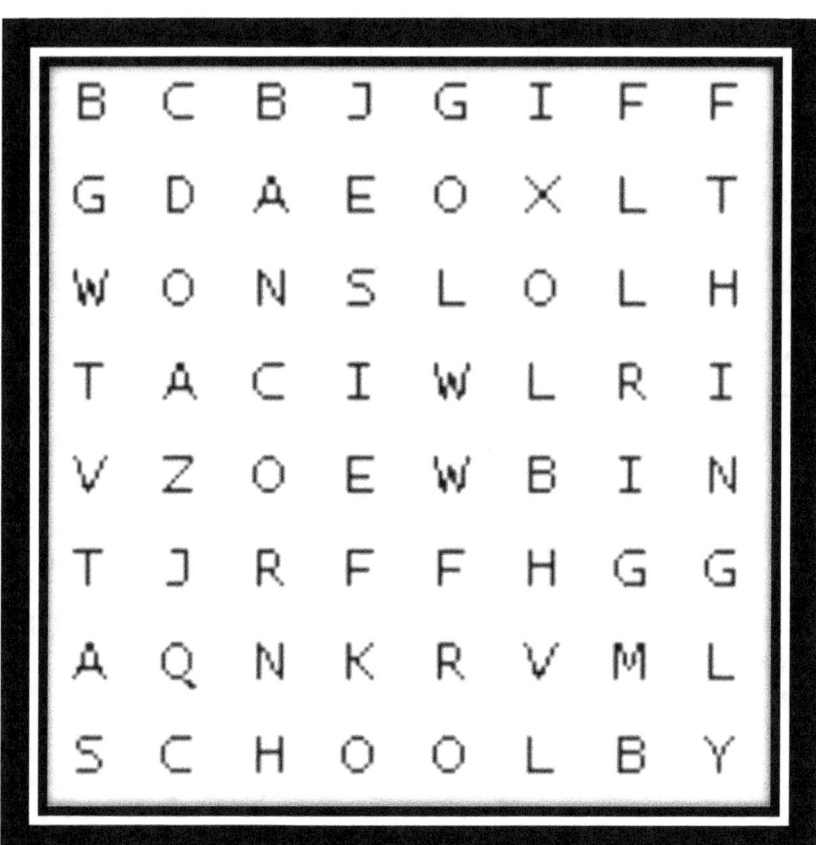

Bell   Cat   Corn
Flower Girl   School
Snow   Thing   Wind

Puzzle #64

Bed
Fish
Man
Squirrel

Claus
Horse
Santa

Door
Leg
Song

Puzzle #65

Ball Chicken Egg
Grass House Kitty
Nest Sun

Puzzle #66

Boat   Car   Children
Morning   Pig   Rabbit
Way

Puzzle #67

Box   Dog   Doll
Duck   Floor   Garden
Window

Puzzle #68

Baby   Back   Bird
Cow   Farm   Hill
Milk

Puzzle #69

Cake   Farmer   Feet
Fire   Mother   Robin
Seed

Puzzle #70

Apple   Hand   Money

Toy

300 Most Common Words
Puzzle #71

About	After	Again
All	Also	An
An	And	Another

Puzzle #72

Able	Above	Accept
Any	Are	Around
As	At	Away

Puzzle #73

Account   Across   Act
Action   activity Back
Be   Because   Been

Puzzle #74

Before   Benefit   Best

Better   Between   Beyond

Big   But   By

Puzzle #75

Bill   Billion   Bit

Black   Blood   Blue

Board   Body   Book

Puzzle #76

Called	Came	Camera
Can	Can	capital
Come	Could	

Puzzle #77

Certain   Chair   Chance

Change   Charge   Check

Puzzle #78

Child   Choice   choose
Day   Did   Do
Does   Down

Puzzle #79

Doctor   Dog   Door
Down   Draw   Dream
Drive   drop   Each

Puzzle #80

Early   East   Easy

Eat   Edge   Effect

Effort   Eight   Even

Puzzle #81

Either	Else	End
enjoy	Fast	Find
First	For	From

Puzzle #82

Father   Fear   Few
Field   Fight   fine
Get   Go   Good
Green

Puzzle #83

Ground	Group	grow
Had	Has	Have
He	Help	Her

Puzzle #84

Here	Him	His
Hospital	Hot	Hotel
Hour	House	How

Puzzle #85

```
P R D W L Y F D
X N H H L I V N
I K J Q J H T A
D E R D N U H B
P Q H I N I U S
H O W U N U M U
R Z J T G H A H
B E O C I E N V
```

How   Huge   Human
Hundred husband   If
In   Into

Puzzle #86

Involve · Is · Issue
It · Item · Its
itself · Job · Just

Puzzle #87

join	Keep	Key
Kid	Kill	Kind
know	Know	line

Puzzle #88

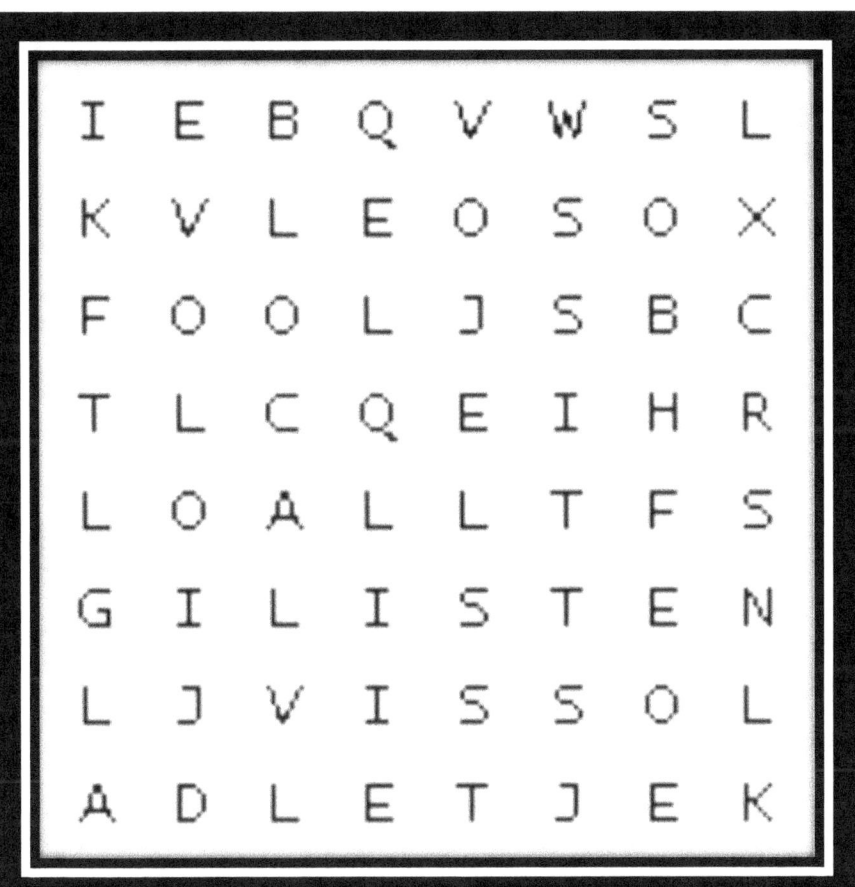

list   listen   live
local   lose   loss
lot   love   low

Puzzle #89

Like Little Long
Look Made   Make
Man   Many   May

Puzzle #90

Me   Month   More
Most   Move   Movie
Much   Must   My

Puzzle #91

New   Next   Nice
Night   No   None
Not   Now   Number

Puzzle #92

Nor   North   Not
Note   notice   Of
Off   Old   On

Puzzle #93

Once   One   Only
Or   Order   Other
Our   Out   Over

Puzzle #94

Outside   Over   Own
owner   Part   People
Place   Pretty   Put

Puzzle #95

```
P P I C I B Q M
P R E V E N T E
Z I I K Y E H L
S V P C C E G B
K A L A E R I O
I T R Q W B R R
B E C U D O R P
Y L B A B O R P
```

Prevent   Price   Private

Probably   Problem   produce

Race   Right

Puzzle #96

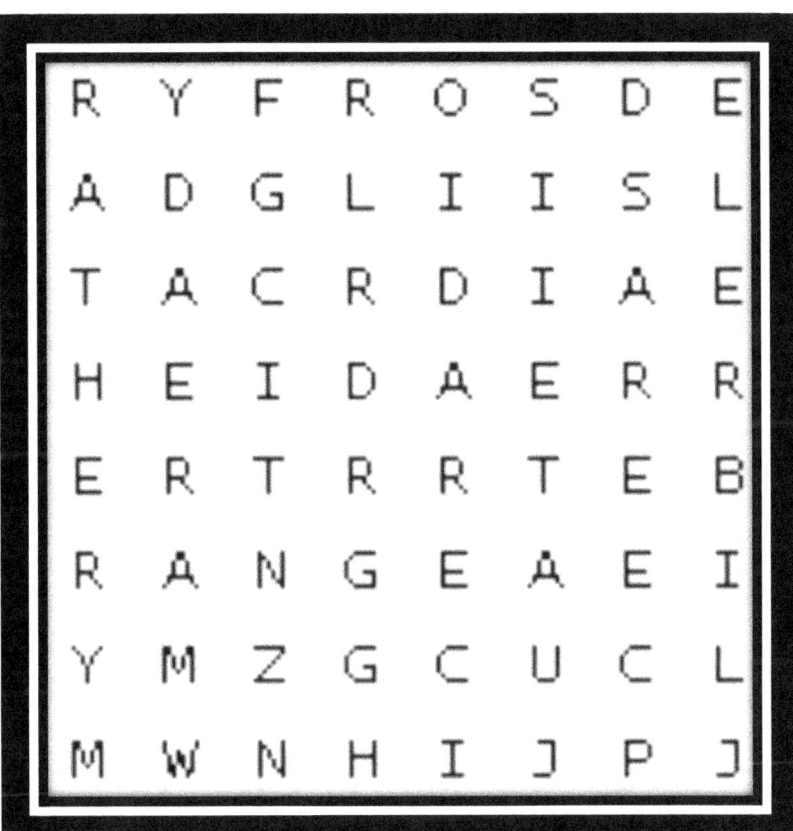

Radio   Raise   Range
Rate   Rather   Reach
Read   Ready   Real

Puzzle #97

rest road Said
Same See She
So Some Such

Puzzle #98

Save   Say   School
Science   Score   sea
Take   Talk

Puzzle #99

Than   That   The
Their   Them   Then
There   These   They

Puzzle #100

Things   Think   This
Three   Through   Time
To   Too   Two

Puzzle #101

Up	Use	Used
Very	Was	Water
Way	We	Well

Puzzle #102

Went   Were   What
When   Where   Which
Who   Why

Puzzle #103

Wife   Will   Wind
With   Word   Words
Work   Would   Write

Puzzle #104

Win Wish Years
Yes Yet You
Young Your

Answers

Pre-K
Puzzle 1

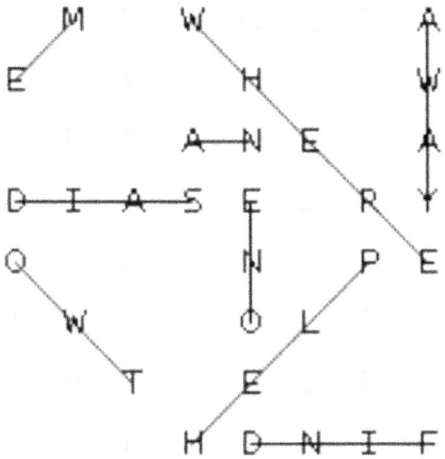

Puzzle 2

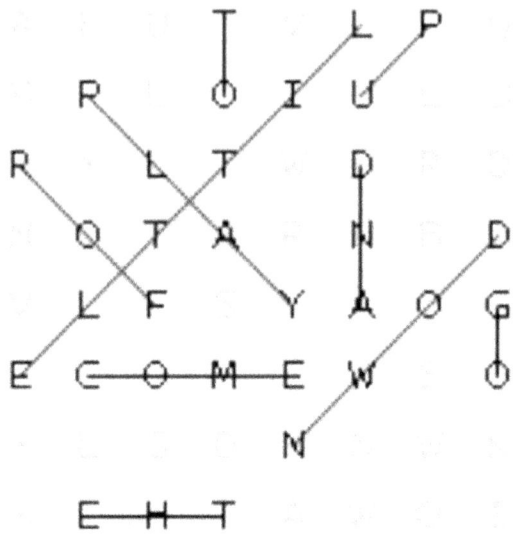

Puzzle 3

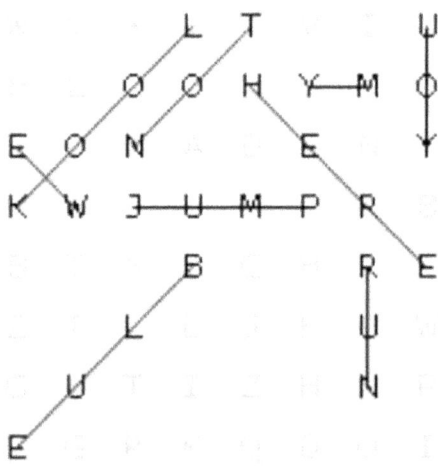

Puzzle 4

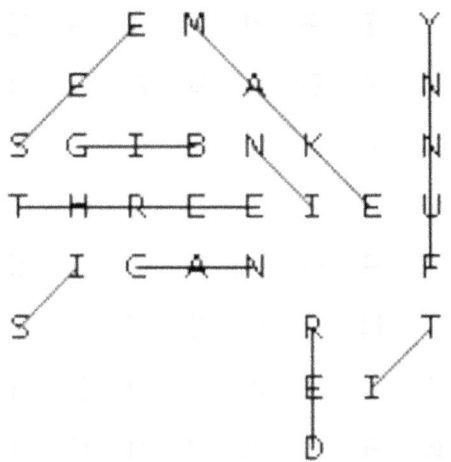

Puzzle 5

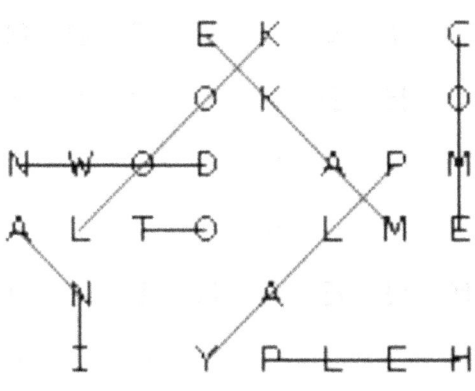

Puzzle 6

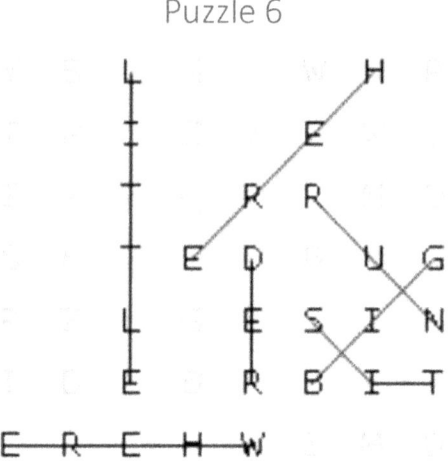

Puzzle 7

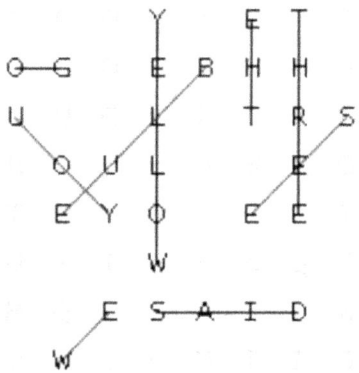

Puzzle 8

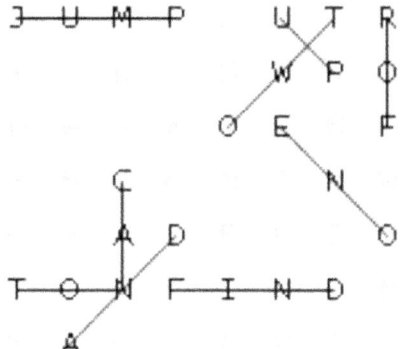

Puzzle 9

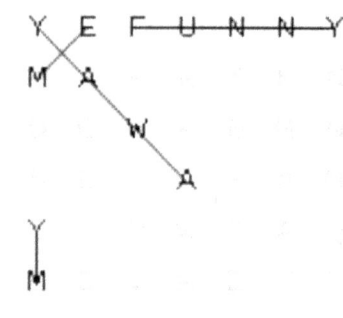

Kindergarten
Puzzle #10

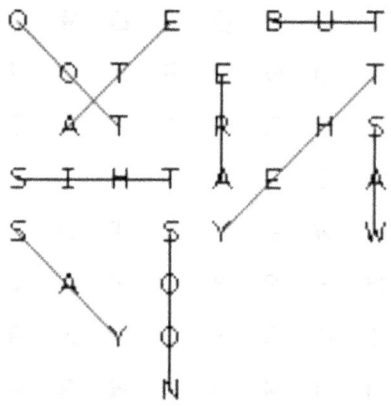

Puzzle #11

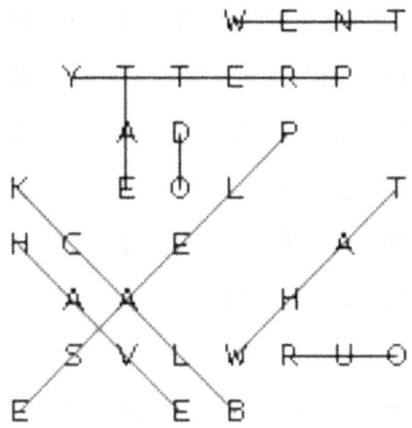

Puzzle #12

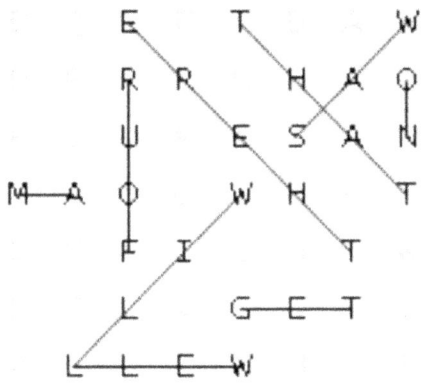

Puzzle #13

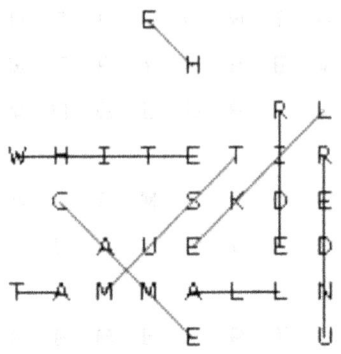

Puzzle #14

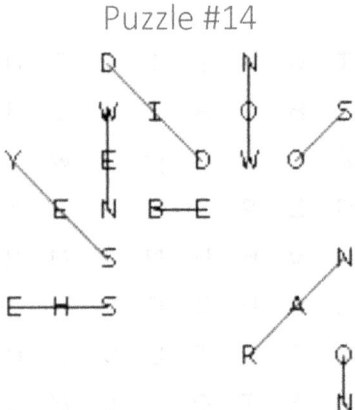

Puzzle #15

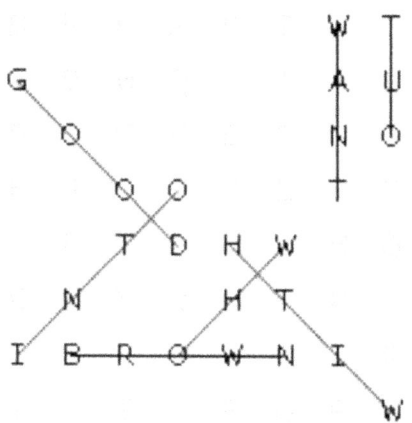

Puzzle #16

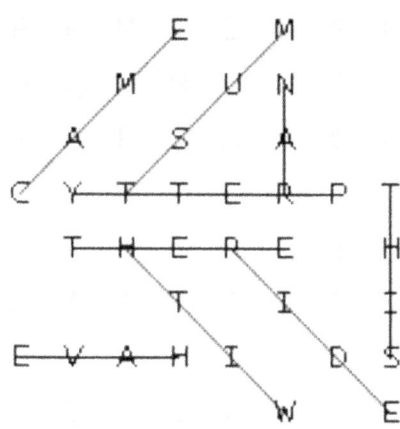

Puzzle #17

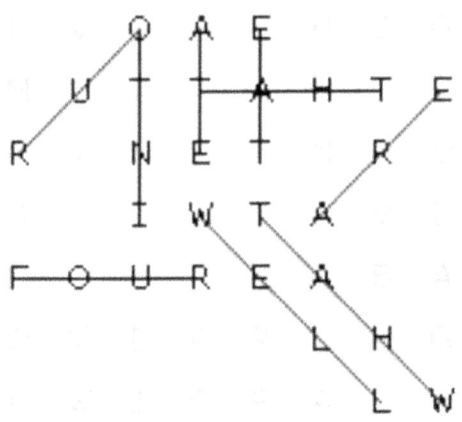

Puzzle #18

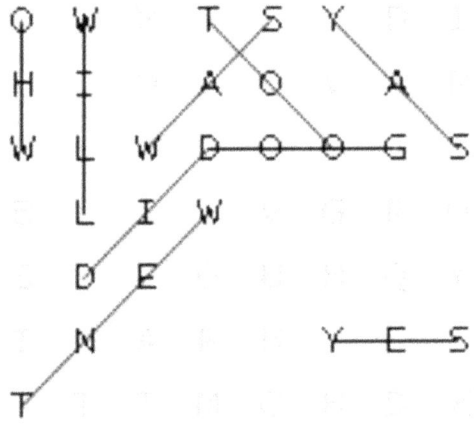

Puzzle #19

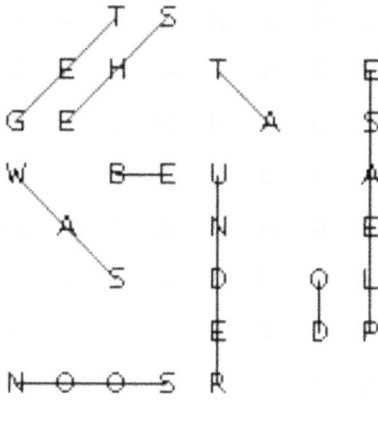

Puzzle #20

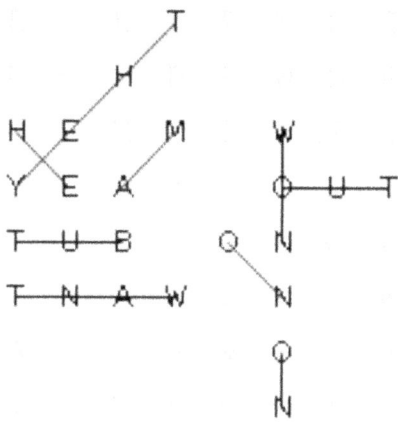

Puzzle #21

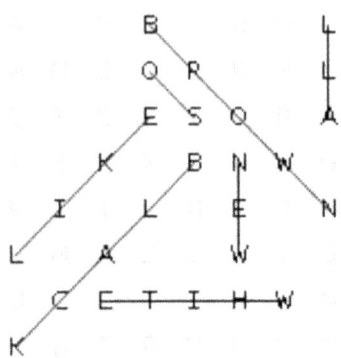

First Grade

Puzzle #22

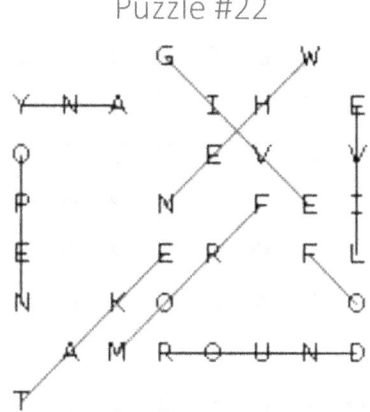

Puzzle #23

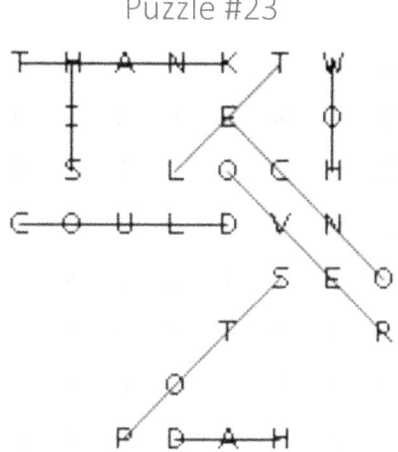

Puzzle #24

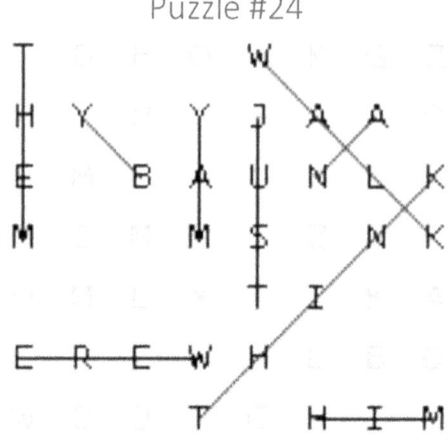

Puzzle #25

Puzzle #26

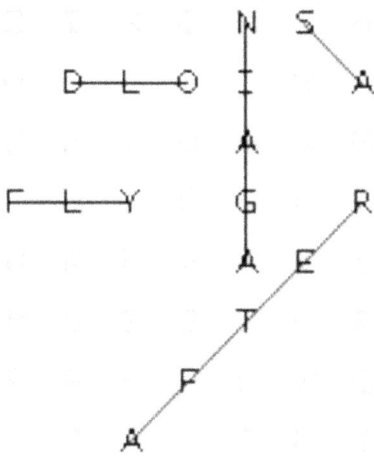

Puzzle #27

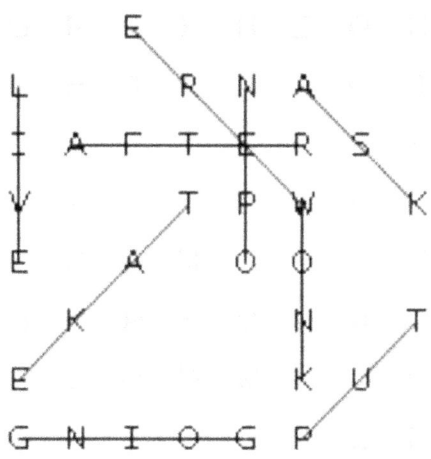

Puzzle #28

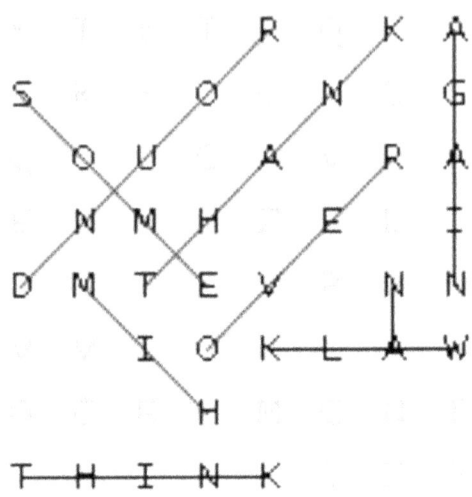

Puzzle #29

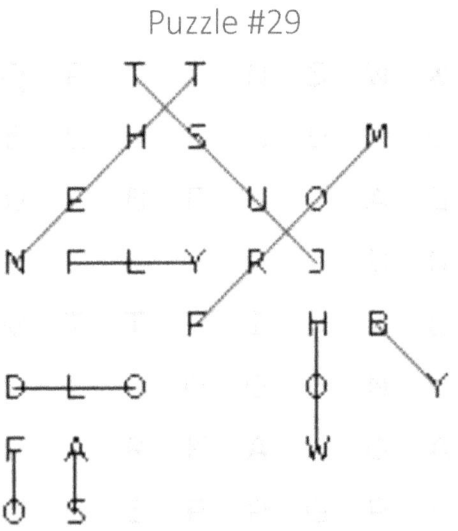

Puzzle #30

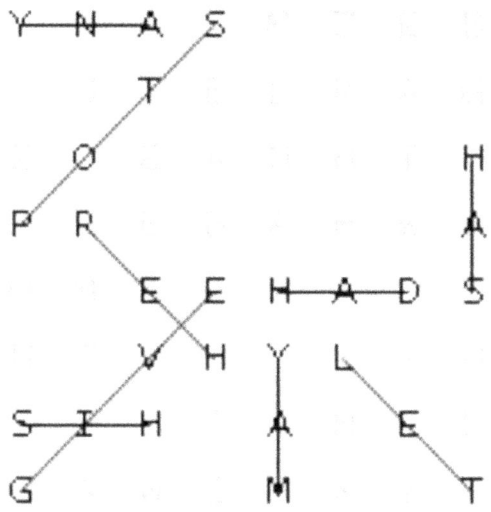

Puzzle #31

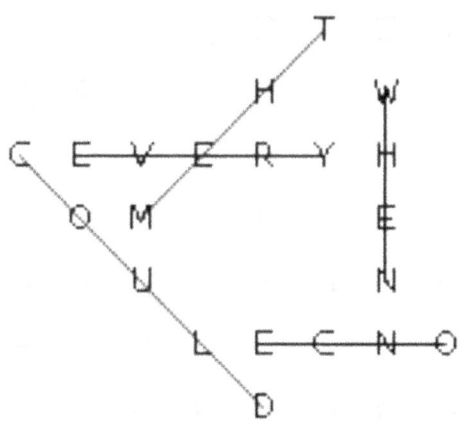

Second Grade
Puzzle #32

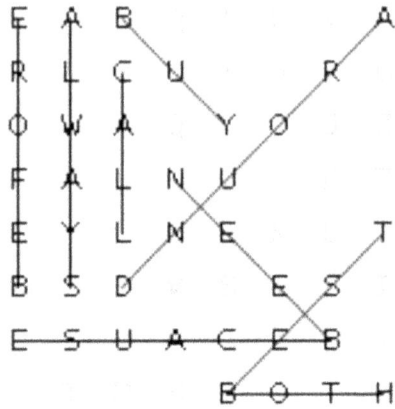

Puzzle #33

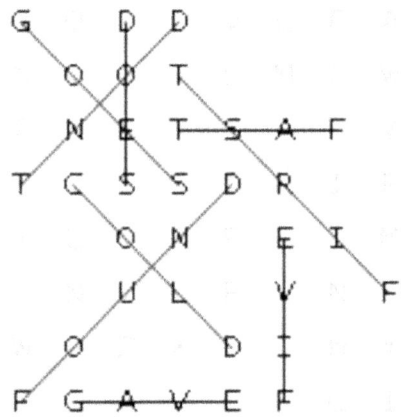

Puzzle #34

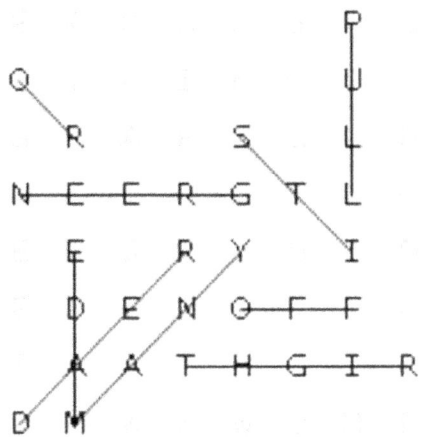

Puzzle #35

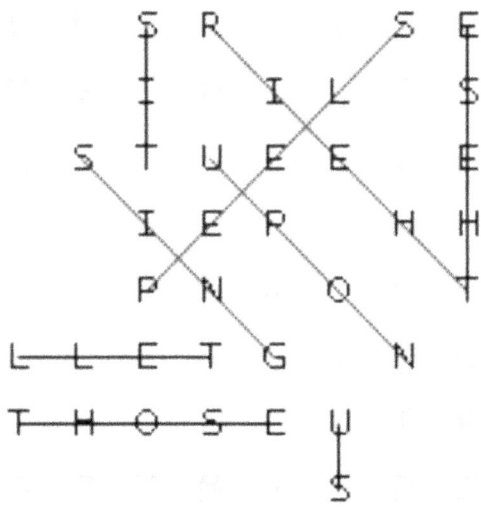

Puzzle #36

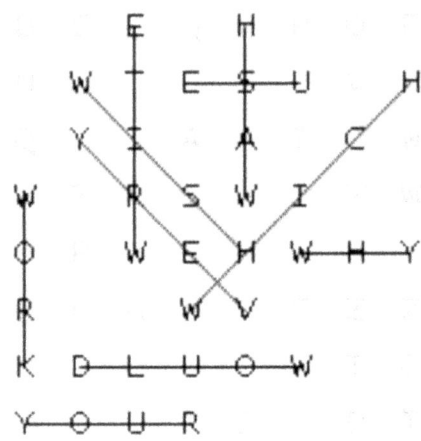

Third Grade
Puzzle #37

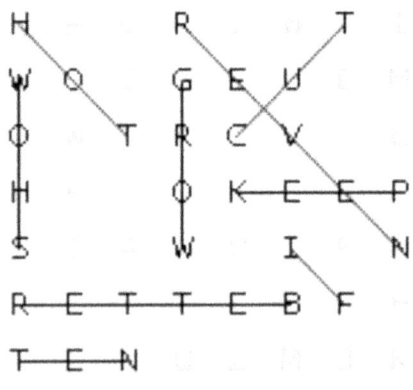

Puzzle #38

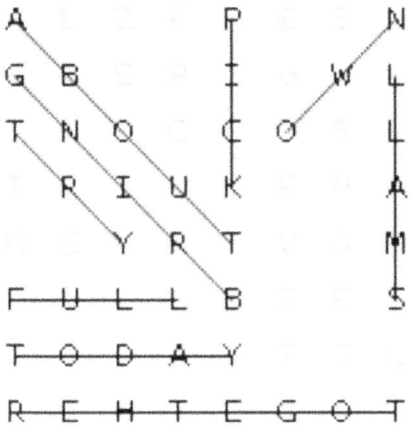

Puzzle #39

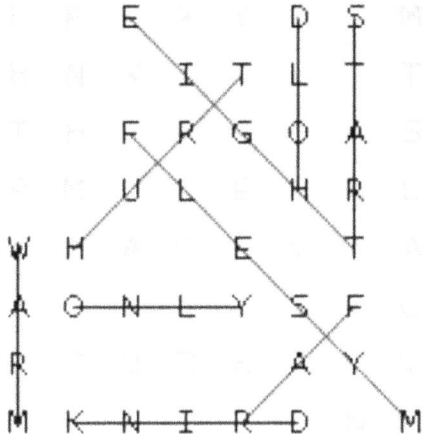

Puzzle #40

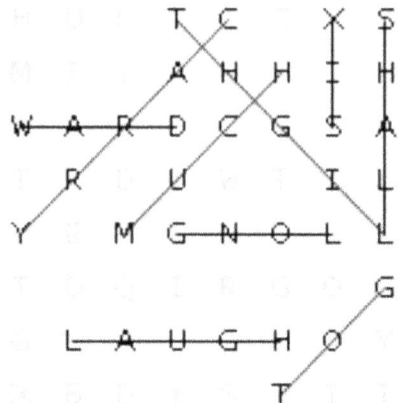

Puzzle #41

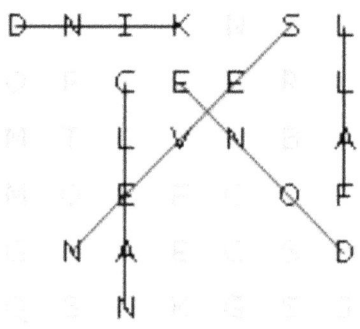

Puzzle #42

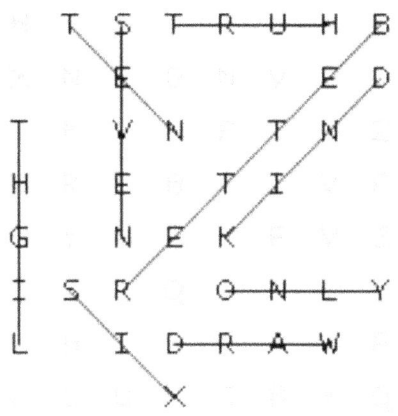

Puzzle #43

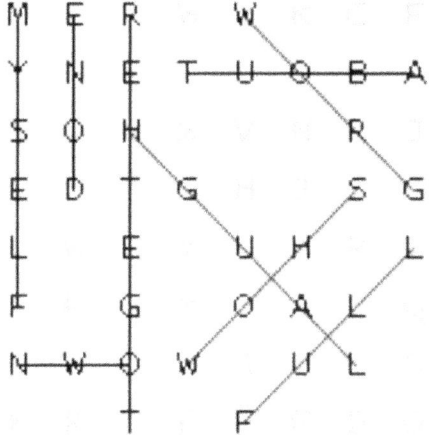

Puzzle #44

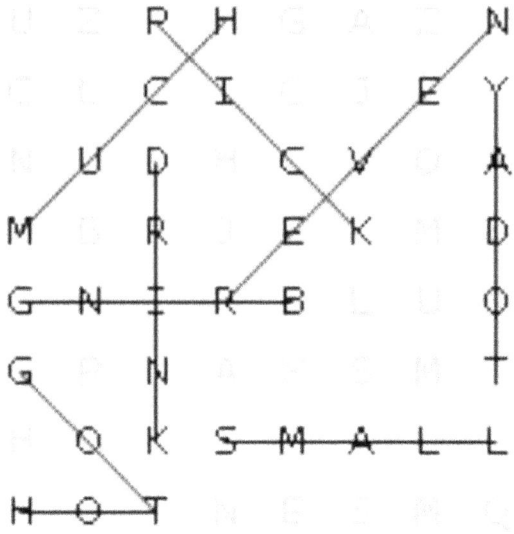

Puzzle #45

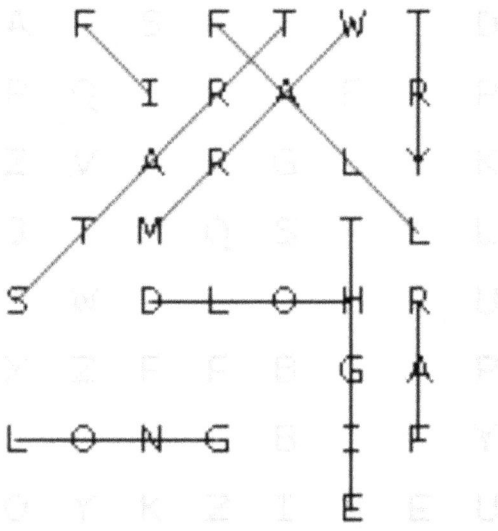

Puzzle #47

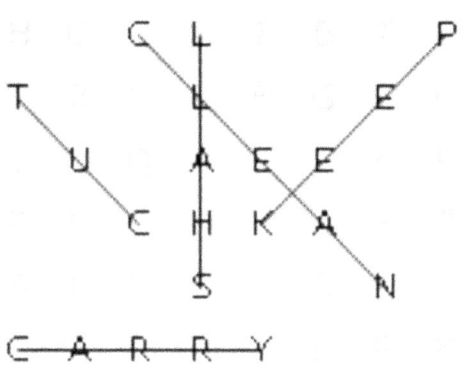

Noun

Puzzle #48

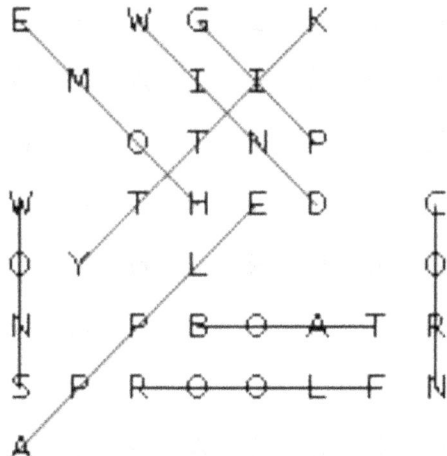

Puzzle #49

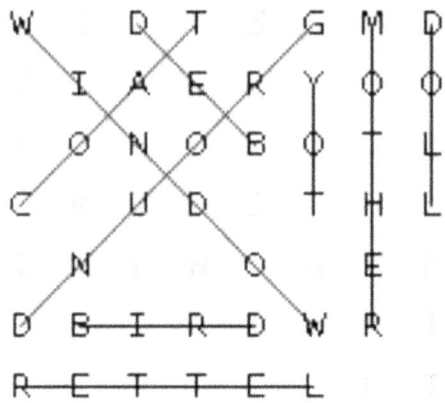

Puzzle #50

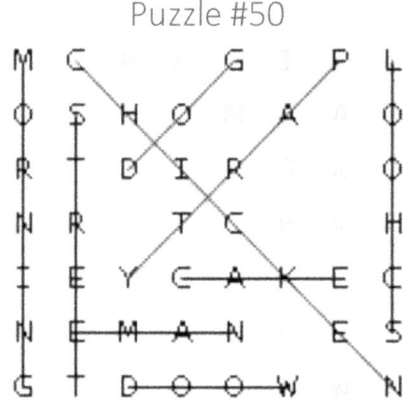

Puzzle #51

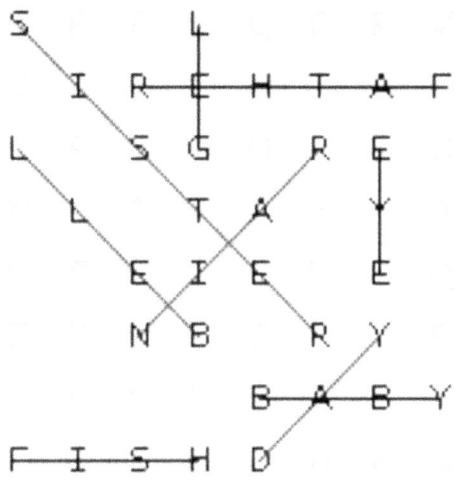

Puzzle #52

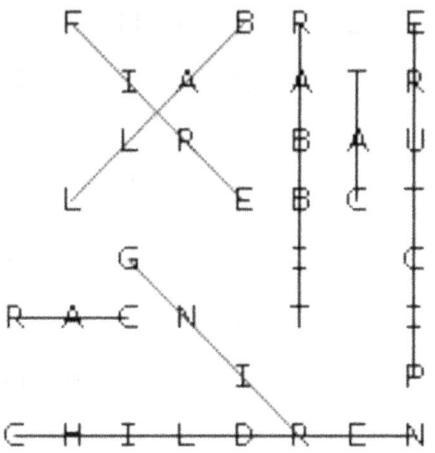

Puzzle #53

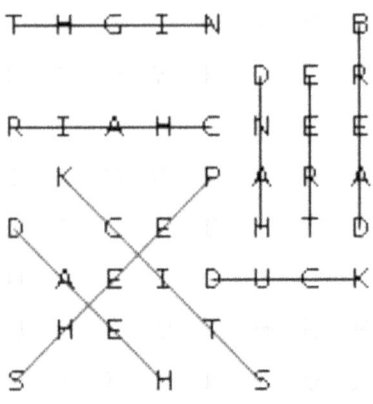

Puzzle #54

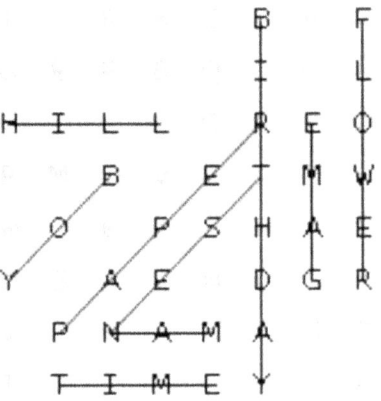

Puzzle #55

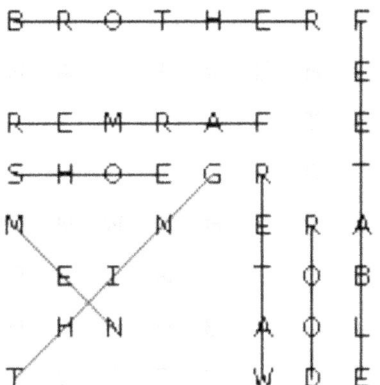

Puzzle #56

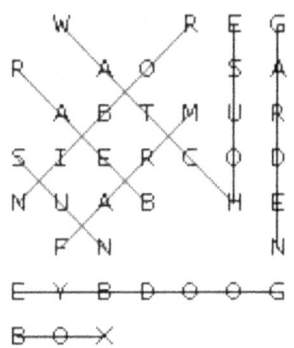

Puzzle #57

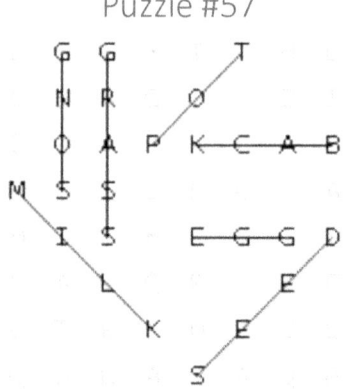

Puzzle #58

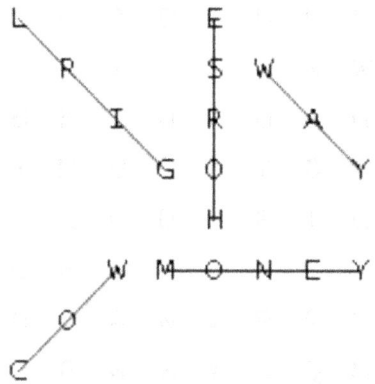

Noun 2
Puzzle #59

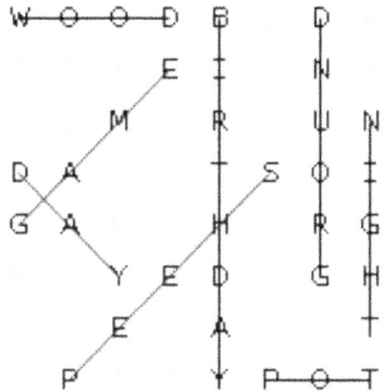

Puzzle #60

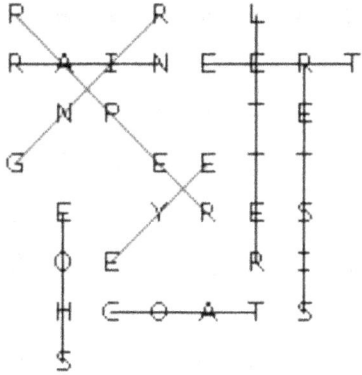

Puzzle #61

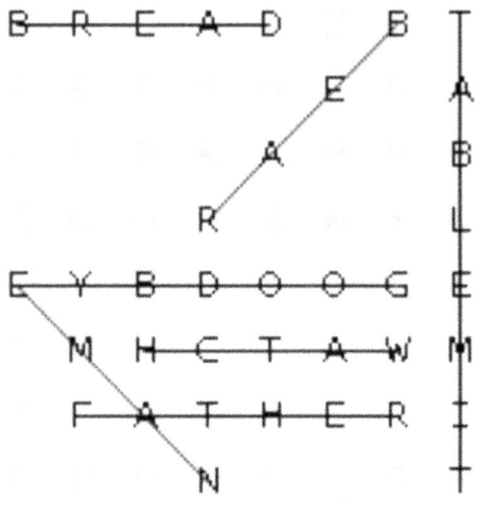

Puzzle #62

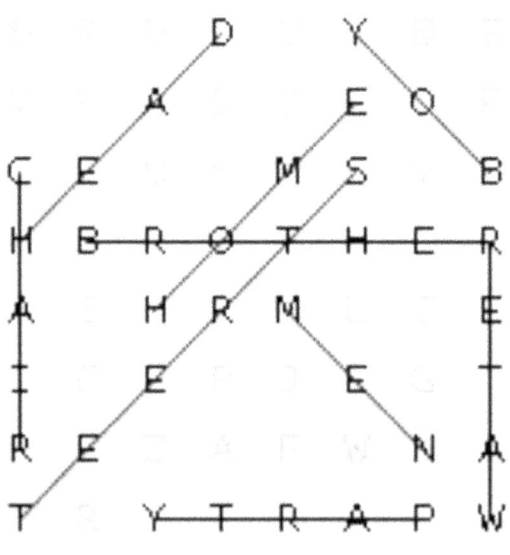

Puzzle #63

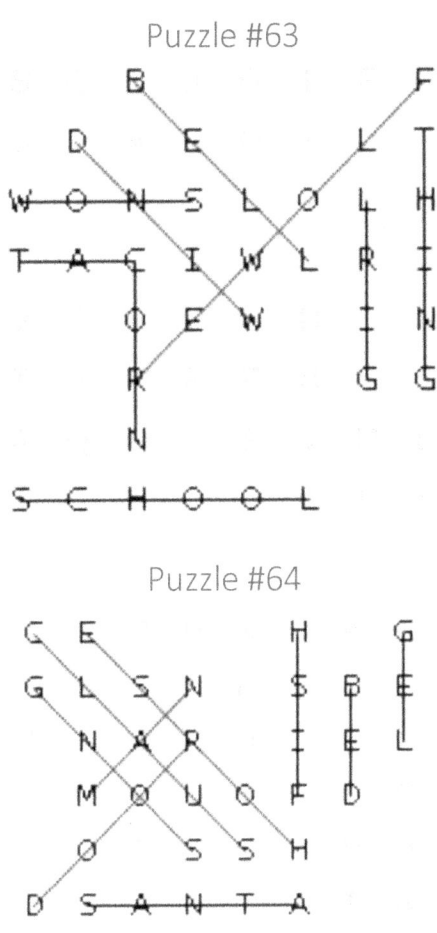

Puzzle #64

Puzzle #65

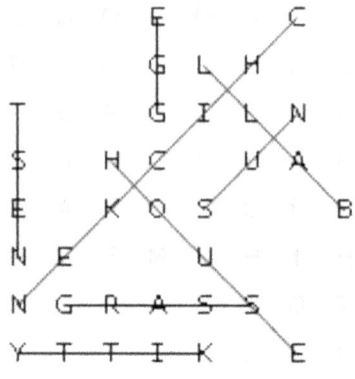

Puzzle #66

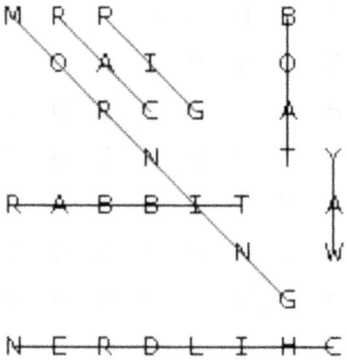

Puzzle #67

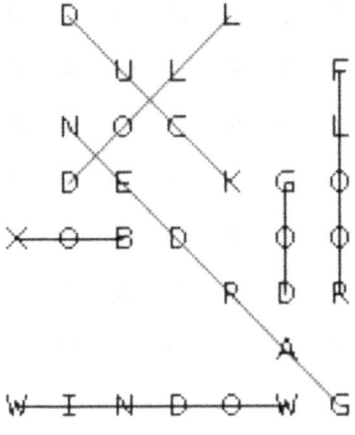

Puzzle #68

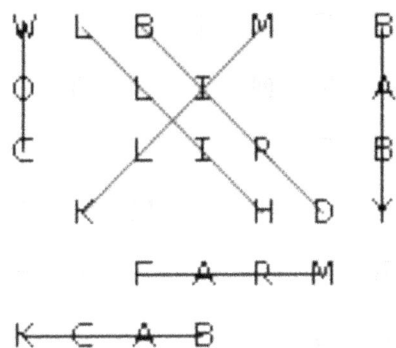

Puzzle #69

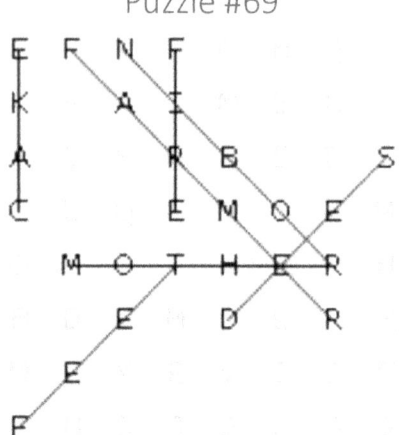

Puzzle #70

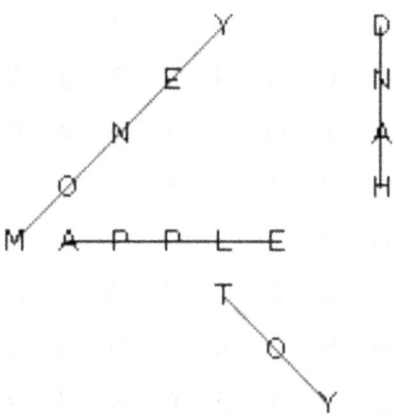

300 Most Common Words
Puzzle #71

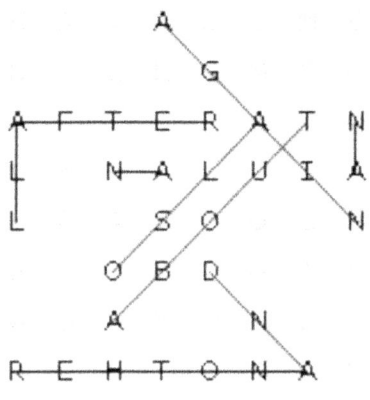

Puzzle #72

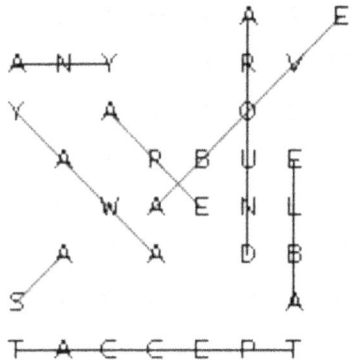

Puzzle #73

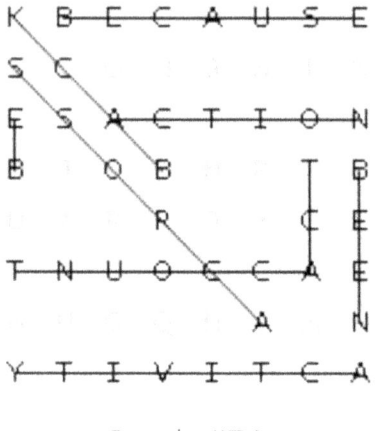

Puzzle #74

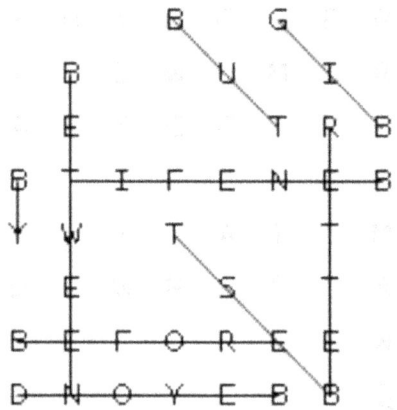

Puzzle #75

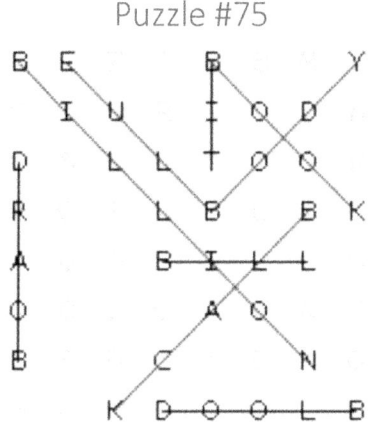

Puzzle #76

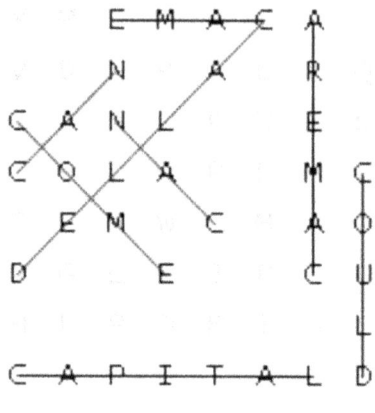

Puzzle #77

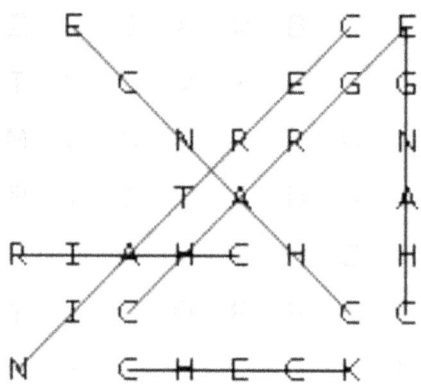

Puzzle #78

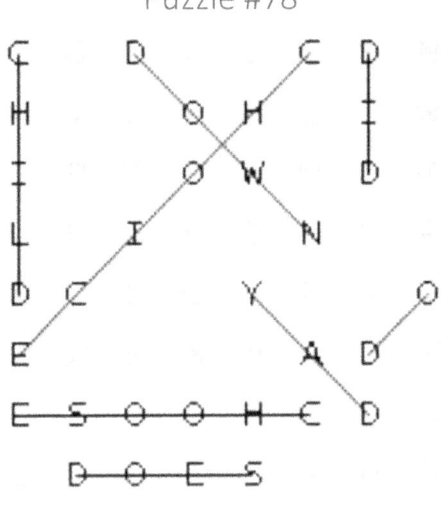

Puzzle #79

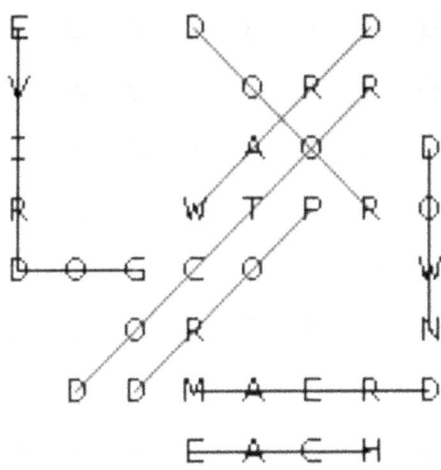

Puzzle #80

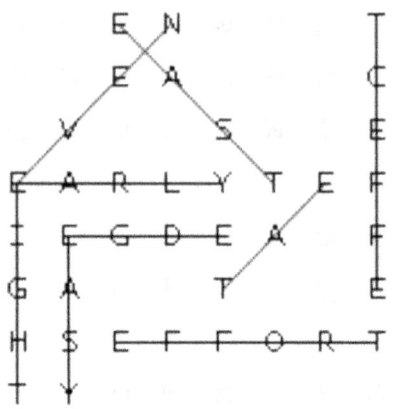

Puzzle #81

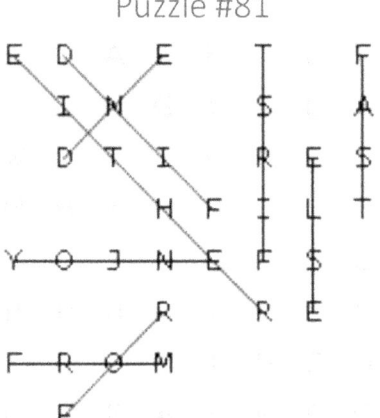

Puzzle #82

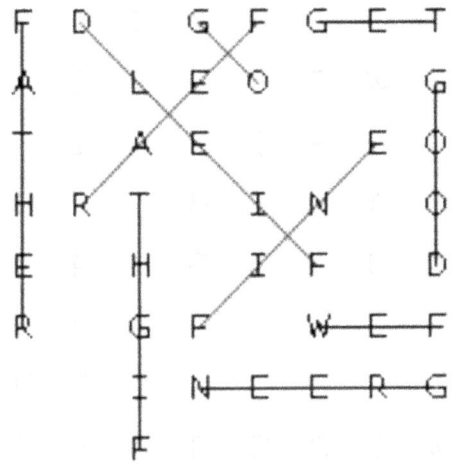

Puzzle #83

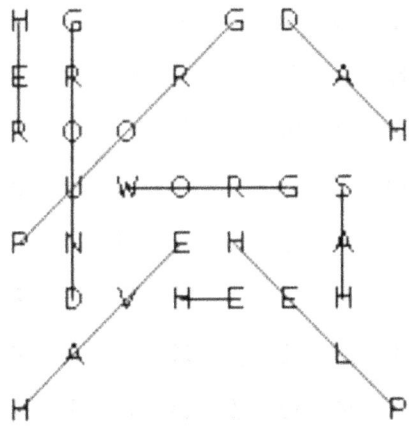

Puzzle #84

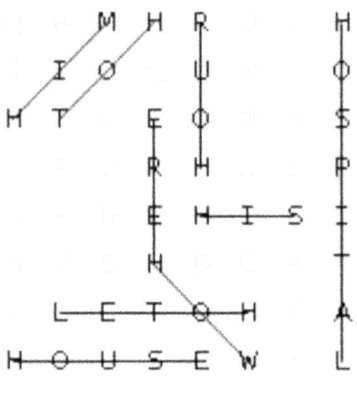

Puzzle #85

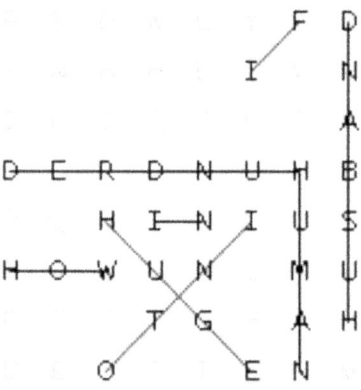

Puzzle #86

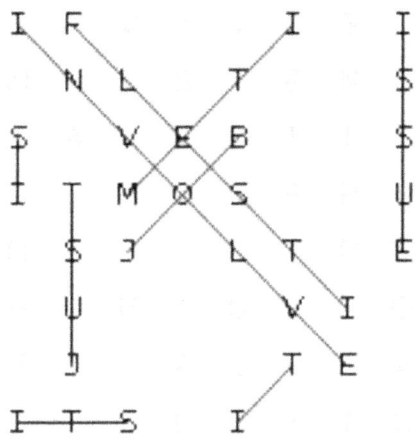

Puzzle #87

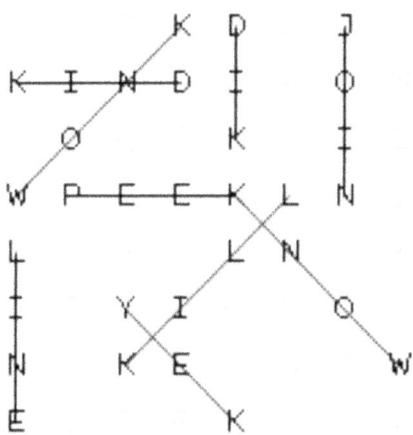

Puzzle #88

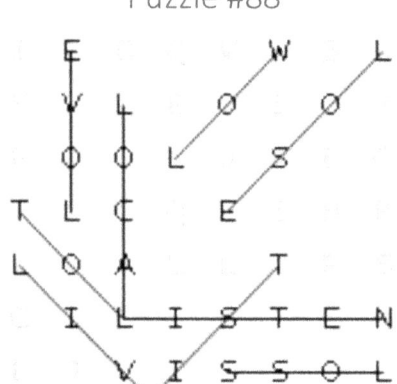

Puzzle #89

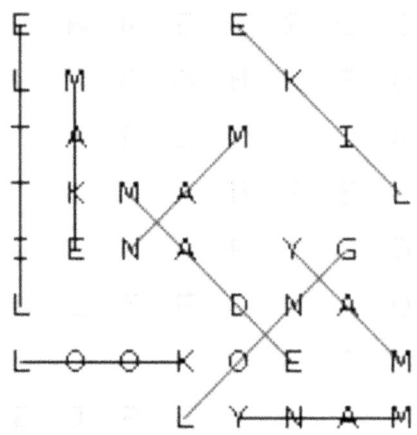

Puzzle #90

Puzzle #91

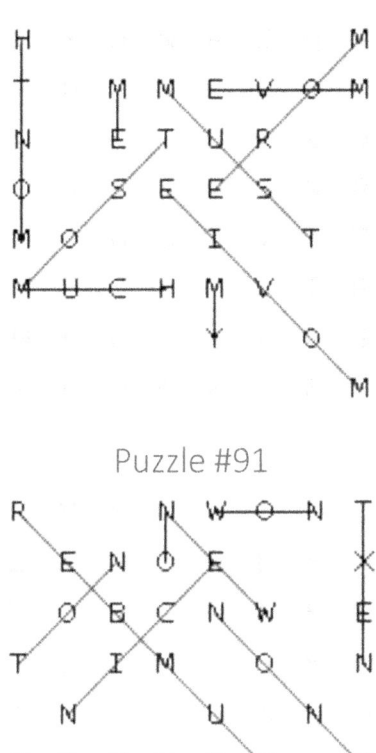

Puzzle #92

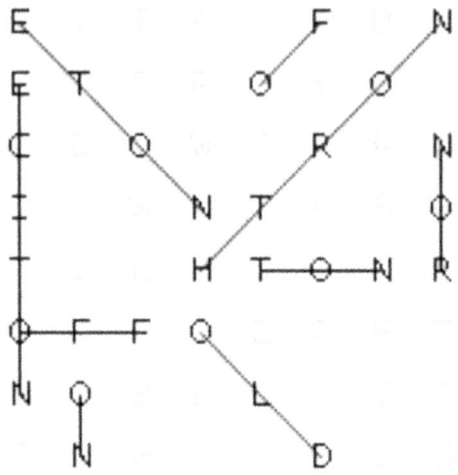

Puzzle #93

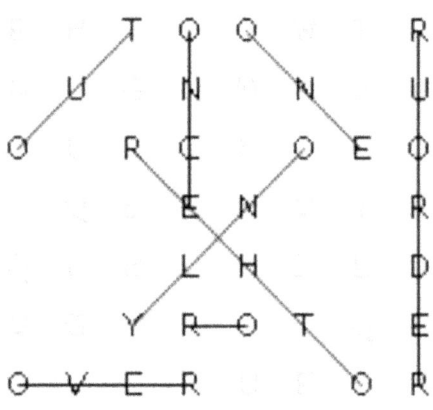

Puzzle #94

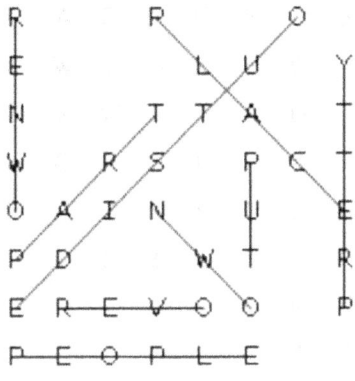

Puzzle #95

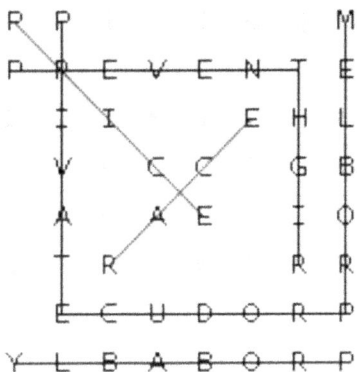

Puzzle #96

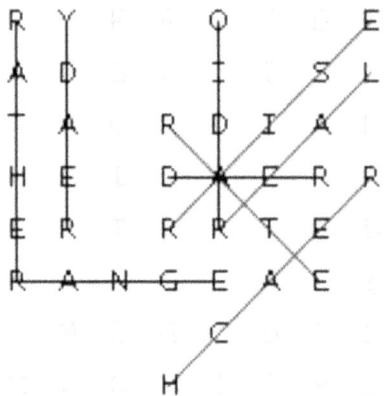

Puzzle #97

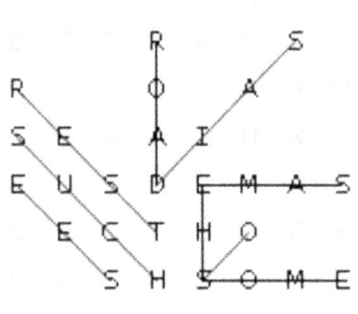

Puzzle #98

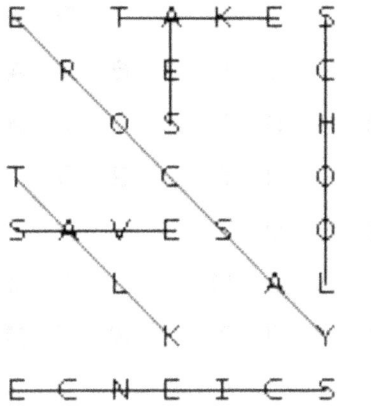

Puzzle #99

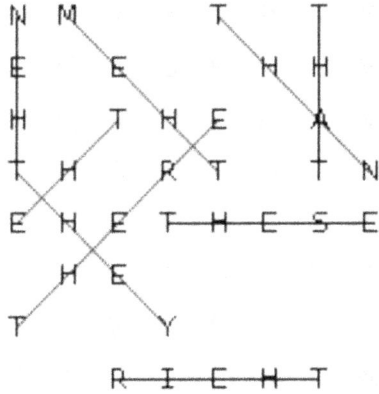

Puzzle #100

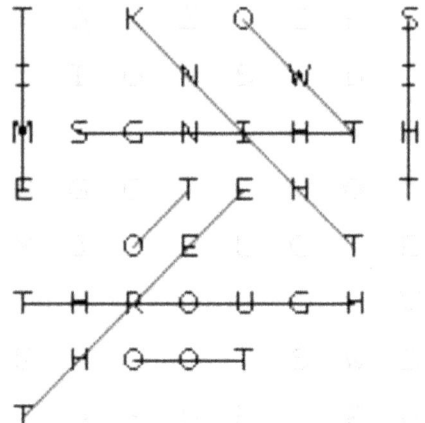

Puzzle #101

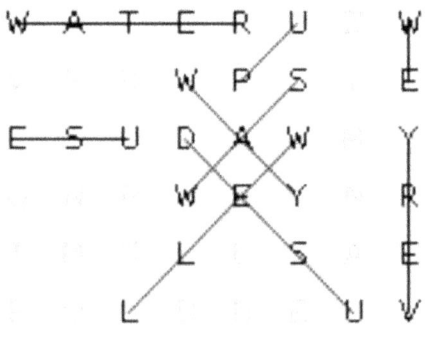

Puzzle #102

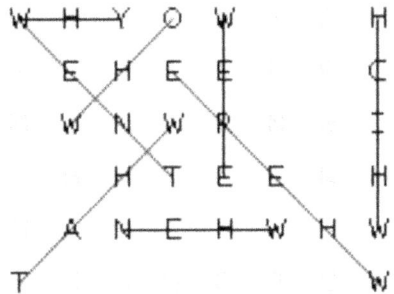

Puzzle #103

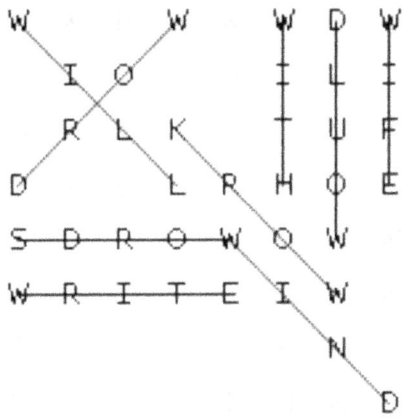

Puzzle #104

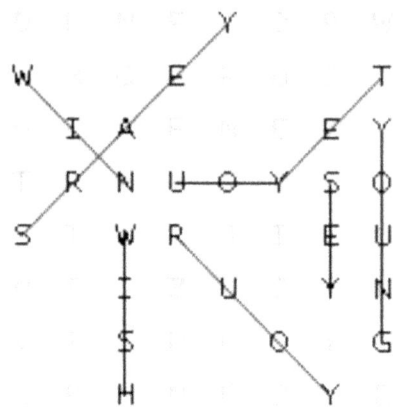

www.ingramcontent.com/pod-product-compliance
Lightning Source LLC
Chambersburg PA
CBHW050236120526
44590CB00016B/2115